Edited by Susanna Sharp Schwacke
Cover Design by Kim Pearson Bolyard

December 2015

Get Out of Your Head or You'll Go Out of Your Mind

Laura Miller Pearson

This book is dedicated to
the memory of my dear husband, Ron
and to all who walk gently
and with reverence on the earth.

Acknowledgements

To Larry Smith, Bottom Dog Press, thank you for your support and encouraging words during the writing of this book. You gave me the courage I needed to finish.

To my amazing children, Kim and Paul, thank you for your continuous support of both me and this book. Your inspiration and consistent feedback was invaluable and I love you both very much. An additional thanks goes to my talented daughter, Kim for all her selfless efforts on both the layout of the book and for designing the front cover artwork.

Table of Contents

1

A Little Memoir of Who I Am

I grew up in western Pennsylvania farm country during the 1930s. I walked to a one-room school for the first two years of my school life, with a row of desks for each grade. Electricity had not yet reached this part of the country, so a tall row of windows lined each side of the class room. If we needed more light than the windows could provide, kerosene lamps were lit.

A potbellied stove sat in the center of the room with a coal bucket close by. This was coal country. There was a table in the back of the room with a bucket of water and a dipper. When it was empty, the bigger boys took turns filling the bucket from a pump near the back door of a farm house down over the hill and across the road. We all had little collapsible tin cups on the upper right corner of our desks. In the entrance vestibule, a rope hung from the bell in the bell tower. One of my dreams was to grow big and strong enough to be able to ring that bell.

I will never forget that school, forever grateful to have had that experience. Most of all, however, I will never forget our teacher, Miss Mary Young. Every single day before we left for home, she read poetry to us. It was the thing I loved most about school. I heard Longfellow, Eugene Field, Robert Louis Stevenson, Whittier and Wordsworth, to name a few.

"The Swing" by Robert Louis Stevenson was one of my favorites and I said it aloud every time I sat down on the swing that hung from a limb of our walnut tree.

> How do you like to go up in a swing,
> > Up in the air so blue?
> Oh, I do think it the pleasantest thing
> > Ever a child can do!

> Up in the air and over the wall,
> > Till I can see so wide,
> River and trees and cattle and all
> > Over the countryside –

> Till I look down on the garden green,
> > Down on the roof so brown –
> Up in the air I go flying again,
> > Up in the air and down!

Miss Young planted the seeds of poetry in my heart where they are still growing. I was and am a child of nature. My favorite place to be was up in a tree. Maybe it was kneeling by the little crick (Western Pennsylvania for creek). Maybe talking to and feeding fuzzy caterpillars. Or just everything and every place in the world of nature.

I was always late for school because I had such an interesting path to travel. The first thing that got my attention was a small gathering of cows right outside our neighbors barn. They always seemed to me watching me so it took me quite a while to move on past them. Then I had a little mud lane to walk down. This was my favorite, because the area hadn't been cleared and cultivated. I forgot all about getting to school on time with so many things to look at and talk to. When I reached the end of that lane, which opened onto a mowed meadow, I still had a little distance to walk before I reached the school. It was then it hit me that I was late because there were no kids outside playing.

I walked even slower, thinking I was in trouble. Bless her heart, Miss Young never punished me. I think it was because deep down inside, she knew that it wouldn't do any good. My mother told me a few years later that Miss Young had once said to her, "Rose, I have never in my life seen a young one move so slowly."

This is how I have approached the writing of this book now that I am in my eighties. As I have grown from child to woman, gained an education, married and raised two children, acted in many theatre productions, taught music and worked in the massage therapy field, among other things, I have sought to move slowly and surely to what lies deep within my heart.

2
This is Me

I am a woman
  a woman with a fire
    a fire in my belly
      and it won't go out.

How is it named
  this fire in my belly?
    Its name is passion
      and it won't go out.

What purpose does it serve,
  this fire named passion,
    this passionate fire
      that won't go out?

It drives this woman
  to write, to speak
    for all of life
      that has no voice.

This fire was fueled
  by the signing of a contract,
    the signing of a contract
      printed deep in my soul.

This contract states:
  all life is sacred,
    all life must be honored
      including my own.

There must be great passion
  to speak for the earth,
    to be heard through
      the blanket of greed and fear.

I am a woman,
  a woman with a fire,
    a fire in my belly
      that will never go out!

3

Get Out of Your Head or You'll Go Out of Your Mind

I refer to the head, that round thing that sits on top of our shoulders, as the Radar Tower. Our minds, like a radar tower, never shut down. The very nature of a radar tower is that it is up and running all of the time and so our Radar Tower Head is not a place of peace. It is designed to be observant, to keep us safe and to alert us to any danger. Consequently, our Radar Tower Head is full of fears and judgments, on tornado alert, so to speak. No peace is there.

My favorite Aesop's Fable is the one about the contest between the Wind and the Sun. The Wind challenged the Sun saying that it could get a traveler to take off his coat. So the Wind blew and blew but the traveler only pulled his coat tighter around himself. The Sun, on the other hand, did just what the Sun always does. It simply sent its warm rays and you know the end of the story: the traveler took off his coat. A wonderful example of power vs. force. The Wind represents force and dwells in the Radar Tower Head. The Sun, on the other hand, represents power and dwells in what I like to call the Heart Territory. Power brings peace and force brings fear in all of its disguises and judgments.

Our Radar Tower Head can get downright noisy at times. When you are working on a project that is not of much interest to you, your mind wanders. Your Radar Tower Head is in the scanning mode. Notice when you are talking to someone, perhaps at a party. You are listening to the person who is talking to you but you are forming the response to the person's comments before it is your turn to speak. At the same time you will be aware of all kinds of things going on in the room, someone's loud laughter, the doorbell ringing and more guests arriving. Smells from the kitchen draw your attention. All the while you are hearing the person who is talking to you. Perhaps your awareness switches to your back that is hurting because you have been standing too long.

The Radar Tower Head is where we catalog all of our life experiences. This is what we were taught by our parents, our religious teaching, what we learned in school. Judgments of all kinds are logged in our Radar Tower Head. A huge part is the self-judgment section. Do we have low or high self-esteem? Do we think we are special or do we feel inferior to others? It can be based on if it was easy to get good grades in school or did we have to struggle to get Cs on our report card. Did we hear criticism at home or were we praised when we grew up, in a poor or rich environment? On and on and on it goes this self-defining judgment.

The Heart Territory, as I mentioned earlier, is our power center, the place of peace. Wild, energetic tornadoes and hurricanes never happen there.

One of my favorite Bible quotes from *Psalm* 46:10 is, "Be still and know that I am God." Now, it doesn't take intelligence to know that it is difficult to feel that peace of God when a tornado is raging upstairs in our Radar Tower Head. However, like the traveler in our fable, there is a part of us that is truly drawn to the warmth of the sun within the Heart Territory. God speaks in the silence of the heart, yet so often we don't calm down long enough to be able to hear it.

Step outside of your house or apartment and take a walk in the world of nature. Open your senses. Nature is an incredible teacher. Notice how plants and trees are instinctively drawn toward the sun. It is encoded within nature as it is within us. Nature does not have a diverting Radar Tower Head as we humans do. When I was little, I remember that we always had a row of sunflowers planted in our garden. They followed the sun's path and always turned their faces toward its glow and warmth.

In the late 80s my husband and I purchased a wonderful home in the Ohio woods. The people who had built the house in the mid 70s had planted a flowering plum tree near the front porch, which looked out over a good sized driveway clearing. The plum tree however, was in shade most of the day. The owners had put strong metal wires on one side of the tree's trunk to keep it from pulling in the direction on the sun. We decided to remove those wires because they had not stopped that tree from leaning. It needed the life giving rays of the sun. We all need the life giving rays of the sun, just as we all need that peaceful voice of God within the Heart Territory. Even if we have several cloudy days, it never occurs to us that the sun might have disappeared. We know and trust that it is simply behind the clouds.

The sun is never "bossy" like the wind. It shines on all without judgment. The sun represents the power of love and the peace of God in the Heart Territory. The wind, on the other hand, represents force and dwells in the Radar Tower Head. With enough of that force, everything in its path is destroyed. There is no healing in force. It is much like harsh judgment and war, and we know that there is nothing healing about war. We need the healing sun that shines down from the sky and that healing sun that shines from that peaceful place of nonjudgment within the Heart Territory. There are many ways to quiet the mind and experience peace.

4
Lesson From the Plum Tree

Now this plum tree planted by the people who had built the house was in the shade. Over the last several years we've had to remove quite a few tall ash trees because of the emerald ash borer disease, so the plum tree was exposed to more sun. In the summer of 2012, for the first time in its life, the plum tree got to stand in full sun. As the summer season changed into fall I was given an amazing lesson from nature. The miracle was unveiled when the autumn leaves fell. For the first time in its life, that tree did not have to struggle to feel the healing rays of the sun. I could hardly believe what I was seeing as I slowly walked to the tree and placed my hand around the limb that was growing straight up out of all those leaning branches. I could feel the power of peace and healing that God quietly shows us through nature. This is a reminder of what can happen when we decide to throw open the shutters of our Radar Tower Head and allow the healing rays of the sun from our Heart Territory to enter.

When I show this miracle to everyone who comes to my house, they stand in awe as they look at it. So many people have asked, "How could this happen?" I encourage them to take hold of that limb and feel for themselves the healing power of nature and the sun. I recall a man who was very tall and physically strong walking slowly to the tree. He gently took hold of that limb, then without letting go he turned slightly, looked straight at me and said with reverence, "I feel the power." The peaceful expression on his face said more than a thousand words.

It is now the summer of 2015 and our little plum tree has doubled in height. There are also many other powerful limbs growing straight up toward the sun. Nature is an amazing teacher.

5
Coming to Earth

We travel to this earth by way of our mother's womb, getting some prenatal lessons, so to speak, to prepare us for life. We begin in this body house, that has all the equipment we need to survive: arms, hands, legs, feet, cardiovascular system, nervous system, just to name a few. As we grow, we become skilled in using these systems. Also, we must not forget to include the "God Wisdom" that is encoded deep in our Heart Territory.

And so we begin our life journey here, enrolled in Earth School University, working on our life PhD. We all have our own course of study that expands as we mature. We travel from nursery school all the way through this university, learning from all of our life experiences. Then with our life PhD in hand, we return to that invisible world from where we came before we took up residency in our mother's womb.

While in this physical form, we need to be sheltered, so we live in our parents' home until we are able to go out on our own. Then we move into a house or apartment that we furnish and decorate to reflect ourselves. Each home will be different from all others. We design it for our own shelter, comfort and safety. From time to time repairs are needed, lawns have to be mowed, or there is a leak in the roof. We gradually learn to adapt and survive in this house that we have made our own. It is like no other house, even if at first glance it appears to be the same as the rest.

Likewise, as we grow from that tiny newborn, we must learn to function in our body houses. We may need repairs and adjustments once in a while as we grow from child to adult. Now our alarm/judgment systems are installed in the Radar Tower Head, which we all need to function, just we need safety devices in any house that shelters us from wind and rain. No two people are exactly the same. Our experiences are different. For example, if two people stand side by side and are asked to describe the view before them, those descriptions will be different, because we all look at things in a different way. We cannot look out at the world through another person's eyes.

We do not need any equipment when we return to the invisible world. Most certainly we do not need our Radar Tower Head. Gone are all of those judgments and fears, that large sum of money, that snazzy car that we thought were so important. They are meaningless in the invisible world. Everyone has a different idea of what that world is, it depends on what we have experienced and learned on our life journey.

6
Dance of Life I

My fantasy as a child centered on being a dancer. I would run and leap with the wind. I climbed any tree that I could get my legs around. I especially loved climbing to the very top of a tree on a windy day. It was a dance. The tree was my partner and the wind was my music. I experienced only joy and freedom high in a tree. I was never afraid because the tree was my world.

I loved storms. One of my loveliest memories as a little girl was sitting in the corner of our back porch, my arm around Prince, our german shepherd, as we watched a raging rain storm. I can see with my mind's eye the twisting and turning of our pear tree caught up in a dance with the wind and the rain. The crashing sounds of thunder completed the drama. My world was nature. I lived there.

Though I had a rich inner world, I had no bridge to the outer. In a sense I had no voice to speak my feelings. I was extremely shy and lived in fantasy. Nature and books were my life. I did not know how to speak about what I saw and felt. This is why I think the arts are so important. Through the arts we are able to get in touch with our feelings and find a way to express them. Great poetry, music, dance, theatre and art are not created in our Radar Tower Head.

When we are touched by a performance or stand before a piece of art, we do not lay our hands on our heads and say, "Oh, how wonderful." Of course not, because we are touched deep within our hearts. I have so often seen or spoken with people, who after a concert, place their hands on their hearts and say something like, "I loved that performance!" Think about it, we only put our hands on our heads when something or someone is driving us crazy so to speak. The arts speak to that place deep within us.

A few years ago, a ballet company from Russia came to our local theatre. It was an incredible experience. The theatre was filled to capacity. There was a hush over the audience as the house lights dimmed and the curtain went up. The conductor lifted his baton and the musicians began to play with one voice. I felt myself transported to a place of wonder as the dancers entered and the story unfolded. Before I knew it, the dancers were bowing and the audience was on its feet applauding and it was time to go home. I felt like I had just sat down in my seat. During the entire performance I never had a thought in my Radar Tower Head. Everything was in my Heart Territory, it was as if time had stood still. As I walked out of the theatre I looked at my watch and realized that I had arrived three hours before. Where had the time gone? In the Heart Territory there is no time.

Please take a giant leap with me back to my college days. In addition to my music studies, I was introduced to the world of theatre. During my four years there I was involved with every musical comedy and drama that my schedule would allow. After graduating I was hired as an elementary music supervisor and high school choral music director. I loved teaching, however the love of theatre was calling from deep within me.

After four years of teaching music I decided to resign and enter drama school in New York City. In the fall of 1957 I moved to New York. This was quite a change from rural western Pennsylvania. I wasn't sure what school would be the best for me. After looking at several possibilities I chose Tamara Daykarhanova's School for the Stage. I made the right choice. She was a wonderful teacher and a very dramatic woman, to say the least. She was Russian and had studied with the great Stanislavsky. As part of the school program, I studied ballet at a studio in Carnegie Hall. I was 26 years old and, though I had danced all of my life, I'd never had a lesson. I will never forget the feeling of trying on my first pair of toe shoes.

During the summer months, I resigned my part-time job in New York City and returned to Pennsylvania to do summer stock at The Theatre by the Grove on the campus of Indiana State Teachers College. At the end of the season I went back to school in New York and found another part-time job. The fall of 1959 was my last journey to New York. It was in October of that year that I met my wonderful Ron from Chicago. We were married in June of 1960, and set sail on an amazing 50 year life journey together. We lived in Illinois, Wisconsin, Connecticut and Ohio. Wherever we were, I was very involved in music, dance and drama. Ron was always very supportive of what I did and took part when his business/ traveling schedule allowed.

Please take another leap with me. We were on vacation in Canada in the early 60s, where I just "happened" to meet an art teacher who lived close to our home in northern Illinois. She taught in a school for perceptually handicapped children. She said, "I am delighted to meet you, Laura, we have been looking for a music teacher. Here is my phone number, call me when you get home." I did just that and ended up working for two years in that school. I would have stayed longer but Ron had a job change and we moved to Wisconsin. How could I have ever imagined that I would be offered a job while on vacation in another country? The dance of life is truly amazing. I learned so much working with those precious children. I am reminded of a line from the Rogers and Hammerstein musical, *The King and I.* In the song "Getting To Know You" Anna sings, "If you become a teacher, by your pupils you'll be taught." In this life journey we are both students and teachers no matter our age. I have discovered in my own life that, the more I listen and observe from the power of my Heart Territory, the richer my experience.

I feel very fortunate because I have had the opportunity to work with all ages, from preschool to senior citizens. When we lived in Connecticut, I put together a workshop called "Religious Drama and Dance" that I presented to church women's groups all over the state. There was one gathering of women that I will never forget because they all had gray hair. How could I ask them to dance? I had been used to working with women who were much younger. I learned a valuable lesson from that phenomenal group of grandmas. They were very uninhibited and loved trying all of the movements, and had no problem creating their own. The oldest participant in her eighties gave me a hug at the conclusion of the workshop and said, "Laura, I have always wanted to throw my arms into the air and praise God."

We loved our seven years in Old Saybrook, Connecticut. I was involved in many musical productions as performer, director or choreographer. I directed a church choir and religious dramas. I did children's programs in schools and libraries. I especially loved working with children. As a matter of fact, I started my own children's theatre in Old Saybrook. There were no scripts, everything was improvisation. There is nothing wrong with using a script, however the reason I love to work through improvisation is because children really learn to listen and respond from their feelings. In the beginning I got only rehashed television programs. Little by little original ideas began to surface. We practiced various techniques, and, for example, I would have them walk or speak according to how they felt. If you were feeling angry, sad, afraid or silly, your walk would be different and your tone of voice would certainly be different. They really had fun with this. It was wonderful to see how they learned to listen, observe and respond to what they heard, saw and felt.

I would often have the children warm up by saying tongue twisters. It is fun to do and really helps to promote good diction, which is so lacking in today's world. We'd begin very slowly and exaggerate the consonants, continuing as we increased the speed.

Once in a while at children's theatre we would invite parents and friends to come watch us perform. The week before the performance we would talk about and try some ideas that the children had. Though working with these children was a very serious commitment for me, there was never any pressure put on them to perform. It was about having fun and experiencing the joy of creating. They didn't have to worry about learning lines. We decided on a story line and who would like to play which character. In rehearsal we might pick out a certain character and, as a group, experiment with ways that the character might walk, stand or use his or her voice. Everyone tried this to see how it felt to be a clown or perhaps a king, then we would talk about how it felt and try it again another way. They really learned to see and feel the difference.

The day of the performance finally arrived and everyone was very excited. The improvisation began and all the children had to do was to listen and then respond to what they heard and saw. They were truly amazing and it was obvious that they loved what they were doing. The audience loved it as well. In my opinion, this improvisation approach can stimulate creativity in many subjects, not just in theatre.

I'm laughing as I think about this next example of how involved children can become in pretending. It was at home with our own children, Kim and Paul, and the three children I was watching for our neighbor, who was Christmas shopping. Paul and Andrew were three, Kim and John were four, and Susan was six.

I said to them, "Lets make some cookies." Of course, these cookies were going to be pretend cookies. When they were a few years older, we made real cookies, but not at such young ages.

With great excitement we got out our pretend bowls and everything we needed to make Christmas cookies. It was a delightful experience and they were totally engaged. We were on our knees in a circle on the floor of our family room. Our pretend bowls and wooden spoons were in front of us plus any ingredient we wished to use. Of course our cookie sheets and all of the Christmas cookie cutter shapes were there as well.

They were very excited as we began putting ingredients into our bowls. They were using their pretend wooden spoons with great energy. We stopped every once in a while and stuck a finger into the dough for a taste. I'd say something like, "What do you think, do we need to add anything else?" Then one might say, "Lets put in some more raisins." Everyone would nod in agreement and throw in a handful of raisins and stir them into the dough with great energy.

Finally they all agreed that it was ready to roll out to make the cookie shapes. That took quite a bit of time because they all had to let it be known what shapes they were using. All of the cookies were gently placed on their pretend cookie sheets. I said, "Now find your oven and put your cookies in to bake." Holding their cookie sheets, they ran this way and that all over the room deciding where to put their ovens. I said, "We'll check them in a little while, we don't want them to burn."

All of the sudden Paul began to sob. I said, "Paul, Paul, what's wrong?" Finally he was able to say through his sobs, "Andrew stepped on my cookies!" He continued to sob. As it turned out Paul had chosen to place his oven on the floor right in the middle of the room. Of course, Andrew never saw it because he was too busy deciding where to put his own oven. Paul was so upset that we had to get into our circle again and make another batch of pretend cookies. After putting the new ones on their cookie sheets I said, "Now put your oven in a very safe place where no one can step on your cookies." They did just that. We all had a wonderful time and pretend clean up was a very easy task for me.

I think you can see why I love working with children. I have had many opportunities to do that in Ohio, where we moved in the early 70s. I continued to put together children's programs for schools, libraries and mother-daughter banquets.

I'd made quite a few costumes that I could slip into very quickly. The children would be gathered in a semicircle in front of me, facing the audience. Perhaps I'd decide to slip into a red polka dot pinafore and black pigtail wig, which took me less than an minute. I'd clap my hands and call, "Toto, Toto! Where are you Toto?" Without fail a little child would come crawling quickly toward me barking. I'd say something like, "Where have you been, Toto? I've been looking all over for you." Then off we would go down the Yellow Brick Road.

Then at just the right time, I would whip off the black wig and pinafore, quickly slip into a black cape, pull a crazy white wig onto my head and pick up an apple. I would walk up to a little girl and say in my most beguiling "witch" way, "Snow White, my pretty, here is an apple for you." Without fail, that little girl would reach for the apple and become one with the character, Snow White. All of the children went right with me into that story. We all had fun and so did the audience.

7
Dance of Life II

Children are the heirs of what we adults leave behind. They are the hope of the survival of planet Earth and all of its families. We are caught up in a frantic web of technology that is like an energetic hurricane gaining momentum all around us. In so many ways this technology storm in our Radar Tower Heads is suffocating all that we hold dear in our Heart Territories of peace. Our precious little ones are being swept along by a tidal wave of technology that is taking its toll. If we want to survive we must wake up from this energetic trance of technology and materialism and take a serious look at how out of balance we have become.

A few years ago Kim and Paul and their families were visiting. The visit happened to coincide with the opening of the sequel to a popular children's movie about cars. Everyone wanted to see the film so we all went. My grandsons were quite young. Kim and Paul said that the original film had been delightful so we assumed that the sequel would be delightful, as well. We were fairly close to the front so that our little boys could see the screen and the theatre was completely full. You could feel excitement in the air as the movie began.

I was shocked to see how vicious and angry those cars had become. I could not believe my eyes. I glanced over at my precious grandsons, who were taking it all in like little sponges. There were many parts of the film that I could not bear to look at. I felt heartsick.

After the film was over, Paul, Kim and their spouses shared the same surprise and disappointment that I felt. It was not the kind of movie that you wanted any child to see yet this was advertised as a children's movie.

The movie industry has become very advanced in technology and can create all sorts of bizarre images. It seems as though not much thought is given to how these images are affecting our children. Scientists around the world are studying the effects on the brains of children and teenagers who are exposed to excessive amounts of television, video games and all sorts of electronic gadgets. It is common knowledge that the frontal cortex of the brain is not completely formed until the early twenties. The American Academy of Pediatrics (AAP) says that studies have shown that excessive media use can lead to attention problems, school difficulties, sleep and eating disorders, and aggressive behavior. They recommend that parents establish "screen-free" zones at home by making sure there are no televisions, computers or video games in children's bedrooms and also turning off the TV during mealtime. The AAP also discourages TV and other media use by children younger than 2 years of age. There is an abundance of information available.

In *The Impact of Television* by Tannis MacBeth Williams, there was a town in central British Columbia that could not get TV because it was situated in a remote valley. In 1973 the town elders convinced the Canadian Broadcasting Company to install a transmitter just for them. Williams, a professor of sociology at the University of British Columbia in Vancouver, heard about the installation and decided to test the hypotheses about the effects of television by looking at the town before and after TV arrived. The studies were done on various grades in the public schools. For example, if students in grade 2 were studied in Phase 1, those same students were studied in grade 4 after TV had arrived. Complete background data on the students was gathered, such as IQ scores, socio-economic status of their families and aggressive tendencies to name a few. Summary: the introduction of television made kids more aggressive, harmed the acquisition of reading skills, decreased creativity scores, and cut participation in non-TV leisure activities.

Earlier I made the comment that we are out of balance and wrapped too tightly in this web of technology. It amazes me, for example, when it is announced that a new electronic gadget has been developed and can be purchased on a certain date. People will stand in line for hours, perhaps even sleep all night on the street, so they can be one of the first ones to purchase that new creation. It has become, for lack of a better word, an addiction. On a certain level, it's almost funny, but the truth is it's very sad to think about how far we fallen from our connection with the wonders of the natural world, which is our source of food, water and life-giving oxygen. It's not unusual to drive down a country road and observe a group of young people waiting for the morning school bus. More often than not they will be focused on their electronic devices. If three bald eagles flew over their heads they would never see them.

I recently attended a gathering of people and had the opportunity to talk to some teachers. One of the teachers at the college level said that many of her students ask if she will put the lessons on the Internet. She has agreed to do that but I could feel disappointment in her voice. It certainly made me feel sad. Online learning is at a great cost.

One of the greatest joys of attending school is to be in a classroom with a teacher who teaches from the heart and opens the door of wonder and possibility. It makes me think of the great desire I had to visit and view the Grand Canyon. I had read all about it and looked at many beautiful pictures. That did not in any way prepare me for actually walking to the edge of that magnificent wonder of nature and seeing it with my own eyes. Online viewing would not even have come close. We need to wake up and wiggle our way out of this technology straightjacket and have a long overdue reunion with the wisdom in our Heart Territories and the natural world in which we live and depend on for our survival.

Our home is in a wooded area with trees lining both sides of the driveway. We have not tried to make a manicured lawn around those trees, so all kinds of interesting foliage is free to grow. It is very common to see both Virginia creeper and poison ivy vines growing up the trunks of trees. My three grandsons came to visit, and I wanted them to know the difference. Aiden and Ryan live in California and Collin lives south of Columbus, Ohio. I pointed out to them that poison ivy has three leaves and Virginia creeper has five. When we looked at a tree that had a vine with three leaves, I would have them raise one hand with three fingers in the air. When we saw a tree with Virginia creeper, I would have them lift a hand with five fingers raised. We walked along the driveway a few times identifying the vines that we saw. Then we made up a little song as we skipped up and down the driveway. "Three leaves poison ivy! Five leaves Virginia creeper! Tra la la la la la....la la la!" Of course, we held up three fingers or five depending on which vine we were singing about. It was great fun and they learned an important nature lesson.

I encourage parents and grandparents to take children out into nature. If you live in the city, perhaps you can find a little park. If it isn't possible for you to find a park, pull into a shopping mall. Maybe you will see a tree that has been planted in a little area where there is no concrete or asphalt. You could make up a story or a poem about that tree. The possibilities are endless. Not only will your children get a break from the world of technology, they will have fun and connect with the natural world – yes, even in a shopping center parking lot.

Back in 1986, I was an instructor in dance and drama with the Caryl Crane Children's Theatre. One of the children in the class told us that they were studying volcanic eruptions at school so we created a dance depicting the rumbling beneath the earth's crust, the explosion and the outpouring of lava. The dance that the children created was wonderful and gave them a different awareness and curiosity about volcanic eruptions.

8
Dance of Life III

One of my favorite things to do has always been putting together one person presentations of women who have had something special to say, such as Abigail Adams, Emily Dickinson and many women of the Bible.

In April of 1980 – we were living in Huron at the time – I walked out to the end of our driveway to collect the mail. On top of the stack of mail was the April edition of *The Lutheran Standard Magazine* and there was a nun's picture on the front cover. I had no idea who it was but I thought that it was one of the most beautiful faces that I had ever seen. I couldn't wait to get into the house to find out who she was. It was Mother Teresa. As I looked at her picture and read the article, I said to myself, "Some day, I am going to do something about Mother Teresa."

In the summer of 1994, I received a phone call from a member of a Presbyterian Women's Association. She wondered if I would present a program on "Women Who Have Made a Difference" for a regional women's retreat. I told her that I would be delighted to do that. They were thinking of having me present several women spending about ten minutes on each one. I began working on the program immediately, placing Mother Teresa's name at the top of my list. The interesting thing was that I could not find any other woman that seemed to fit with her. I called the woman back and told her that I would be doing a presentation of only Mother Teresa.

I read every book that I could find on Mother Teresa, including some wonderful little books of prayers and wisdom that she herself had written. The more I read the more she inspired me. She was a perfect example of what one person can do from the peace and power of God in the Heart Territory. It was a joy to put this program together. I began by sharing some information about Mother Teresa as I did a makeup change in front of the audience. I made a white sari headdress trimmed in blue that I draped over my head, and then turned and walked to the podium as Mother Teresa. When I turned around to face the audience, we were in Calcutta.

One of my favorite quotes from Mother Teresa is this: "Each individual person has been created to love and be loved, doesn't matter race, doesn't matter religion. Every single man, woman, child is a child of God, created in the image of God, and that's what we look at." With all of the turmoil and fighting that is going on in our world today, Mother Teresa's message of peace and love is needed more than ever. I feel blessed to be carrying her message to all who wish to hear it.

9

Composting

As in all of my writing and work, I use examples from the world of nature. Think about entering a classroom and listening to an amazing teacher named nature. In this class you will have no tests or report cards. All you have to do is listen. Leave your gadgets and smart phones at home and find a quiet place in the natural world. If you do not live in a rural area there are many metro parks that you can visit that have walkways through forests. As you go, listen and observe without judgment. You will experience a deep feeling of peace as you step into that natural world. Among other things look at the floor of that forest as you walk. You will see signs of life growing and blooming, depending on the season.

Take a look at all of those trees that in the fall of the year will drop their leaves and prepare for winter. No one comes in to rake those leaves that drop to the ground. Nature knows how to recycle them without any help from human beings. Without any sound whatsoever, those leaves are changed into soil. This is called composting.

When I was a little girl I loved walking around the farm with my grandmother who taught me about the importance of composting. She always added soil from those compost piles to both her vegetable and flower gardens. Her gardens were beautiful.

The miracle of composting is that it is so quiet. You can stand beside a compost pile – which I have done many times – and you hear absolutely nothing. Yet nature is working nonstop on all of those peelings, leaves, and clippings that have been tossed onto the pile. The soil that nature makes is beautiful, rich and a joy to work with, ready to grow anything.

Let's take a look at what I like to call our energetic compost pile, that each one of us has encoded deep within the Heart Territory of our body house. This is the place of peace, where it is possible to compost all of that "judgment stuff" from the Radar Tower Head of force. No composting goes on up there. I compare this to a cluttered hall closet in your house that is packed full of stuff. Every time you open the door you say to yourself, "I've got to clean that closet!" But so often we shut the door and walk away, just as we do in our Radar Tower Heads which contain a lot of clutter, if we are willing to take a close look. Perhaps I should say, "a close listen."

This is when we have the opportunity to make some life-changing choices. Take a good listen then to what is driving you crazy up there and make a decision to clean that Radar Tower Head closet. All of that "judgment stuff" can be tossed onto the energetic compost pile in our Heart Territory to be converted into a beautiful soil of compassion, peace and healing. As in nature's composting, no sound can be heard, only peace is experienced.

God speaks in the peace and stillness of the Heart Territory. It is difficult to feel peace and to hear the voice of God when we are caught up in the wind and force of our Radar Tower Head. Please, come with me to the crucifixion of Christ in the twenty third chapter of *Luke*.

I have spent much time in prayer concerning these thoughts that I am about to share with you. In my mind's eye I have traveled often to the crucifixion, imagining what it would feel like to witness that angry crowd that was intent on crucifying Jesus Christ, the Prince of Peace. He was nailed to the cross that was raised for all to see. With great sadness I have looked up at Christ's outstretched arms, revealing the power of His open heart. I have truly prayed and prayed about this moment.

One day an amazing thing happened. As I stood there in my prayer meditation asking for guidance, Christ's heart seemed to open before me when I heard him say, *Luke* 23:34, "Father, forgive them, for they know not what they do." I had heard and read those words many times in my life. This day, however, I felt as if my heart was cracking open. I was hearing those words in a deeper place of understanding within my heart. I saw that Christ was looking from His heart into the hearts of those who were jeering and deriding him. They, on the other hand, were looking at him from the prison of their Radar Tower Heads. Their hearts were in lockdown. It hit me that it would have been impossible for them, in their raging storm of judgment and anger, to hear Christ's words let alone be able to understand them. This was something that I know deep in my heart that I needed and wanted to understand. God speaks in the silence of the heart and we are able to hear and to listen when we make the decision to do some compost cleaning in our noisy Radar Tower Heads of judgment.

This truly was a life changing experience for me when I opened my heart and not only heard but felt Christ's words deep within me. A great heaviness seemed to lift from my body that allowed those words to imprint my heart. "Father, forgive them, for they know not what they do." When I see violence or inappropriate behavior among people, I see and feel it in a different way. It makes me very sad rather than angry and it has made me realize that one of the challenges of life is to learn how to forgive those who respond with anger and force in all kinds of situations. That does not mean to condone what has been done – far from it – but to see it in a different and enlightened way.

If we wish for a world of peace we must find a way to open our hearts and reach out with an extended hand of peace rather than a clenched fist of force. More often than not, if someone says or does something against us our first reaction is anger or retaliation. I used to have a poster that read, "It is not the first angry word that causes the quarrel, it is the second angry word." If we are on the receiving side of that first angry word we can choose to respond with a gentle word. This is one of the challenges of being a human being on this earth.

Verse 34, in the twenty third chapter of *Luke*, has touched my heart for as long as I can remember and helped me to understand what it means to forgive. Of course, we know that God forgives us, but aren't we to learn from Christ how to forgive others? I think of "The Lord's Prayer" that says, among other things, "Forgive us our trespasses as we forgive those who trespass against us." We are grateful for the first part of that statement but perhaps too often we ignore the second part, our part. We have some forgiving to do as well, don't we?

Let's go way back in time to the prophesy in the ninth chapter of *Isaiah*, that says that a baby would be born and that among other things, he would be called the Prince of Peace. With the birth of Jesus Christ, God came to us in human form. It became possible for us to have a personal and loving relationship with God deep in our hearts, that place of nonjudgment within all of us. Why then are we still so far away from peace on this earth?

It is about fear and judgment, isn't it? "We have nothing to fear but fear itself," has been attributed to Franklin D. Roosevelt during World War II. As a little girl I did not know what that meant. I do now. It is being played out all around us. Violence and war spring up around us like weeds in a neglected garden. Everywhere we look – in our schools, athletic competitions, politics, corporations, television programs, video games, children's toys, between countries, – we see violence and unrest. Where is that peace that we say we want, even as we are figuring out ways to amp up security all around ourselves and in so many ways teach war? Even in religious institutions there is unrest. It is time to throw open the shutters of our Radar Tower Heads and start tossing all of that "fear stuff" onto our energetic compost piles, where the soil of peace, forgiveness and compassion are created.

"There is no way to peace. Peace is the way." Those words were spoken by Mahatma Gandhi. Look back at what he accomplished with-out violence. He simply stood his ground in his Heart Territory of power and peace. Take a look at the amazing life journey of dear Mother Teresa, who said, "The only cure for the ills of this world of ours is love, the love of God working through us." Who can ever forget Rosa Parks, who quietly sat down in a "whites only" seat on a bus in Montgomery, Alabama? Think about the life accomplishments of Nelson Mandela. He showed us what is possible if we decide to reach out with the an open hand filled with peace and forgiveness that comes from the power of God in our Heart Territory. These four people have shown us what is possible when peace is more important to us than war.

Think about looking up at the power of the Son of God, in the midst of his crucifixion opening His heart and showing us the way of peace, love and forgiveness. It is not easy to forgive someone who has mistreated or deceived you in some way, is it? Also, there are times when we need to take a look deep within ourselves, which is not an easy thing to do. It is much easier to point a finger at someone else, however when we do that, our thumb is pointing back to us. Learning to forgive is one of the lessons that Christ is giving us from the cross. In composting in the Heart Territory we are able to forgive and spread the soil of peace and compassion. It is then that we will truly experience the peace of God that passes all human understanding.

To end this Composting chapter, I'd like to return to nature's classroom. Though it may seem frivolous, the underlying message that I want to communicate is very serious. We were living in Huron, Ohio and our children were in junior high school. We did not have a good place for an outside compost pile, so when I heard about composting inside with containers of soil and "live in" earthworms, I was delighted.

By now, I'm sure you have discovered how much I love everything about nature. I bought a couple of very large containers, put them in the basement and filled them with soil and some earthworms that I purchased from a fishing bait shop. Our daughter, Kim, thought it was great fun. Our son, Paul, was horrified at first and said, "Mother, please don't tell anyone that you are doing this." He was afraid that his friends would tease him about having worms in our basement. My husband, Ron, was fine with the idea if it made me happy. So we were "off and composting."

Those little worms loved every peeling that I placed in that soil and they never made a sound as they worked. Their favorite food was watermelon rind, which they devoured with amazing speed. We all had a good laugh over that. I'd bury some one day and the next day you could not find a trace of that rind. Those worms ate, multiplied and produced wonderful soil that I was able to use for growing sunflower and buckwheat sprouts, among other things, which we enjoyed all year round. After soaking the seeds in water, I planted them on an inch deep layer of the composted soil spread out on cafeteria-size trays. I placed them in our family room which had many windows. In no time at all, they were two inches tall and ready to eat. They were delicious, nutritious and enjoyed by everyone in the family. After I harvested the sprouts I put the used soil roots back into the containers for the earth worms to compost. It was amazing how quickly those worms multiplied and, when it got too crowded, I would take some of them outside and put them in our woods or our little garden. They never seemed to mind wiggling into a new territory.

Nature is an amazing teacher from whom we can all learn, if we decide to pay attention. It is essential for our survival that we take a look at what is happening to our beautiful earth. Among other things, look at the plastic that is being used in such abundance and is so thoughtlessly and casually tossed into the landfills. Wonderful little earthworms are not equipped to compost plastic! Talk about "a fist in the eyes of God." We must wake up before it is too late. I carry my own reusable cloth bags with me when I go shopping. As a matter of fact, I have a stack of them in the back seat of my car. Quite often I gently suggest to people that perhaps they make or buy some special bags for shopping. Many times someone will laugh and say, "Oh, I know, I have one but I always forget to take it along." I say to myself that we don't forget the things that are important to us, do we?

Not long ago, I was talking to a young woman who works at a local garden center. She has been trying to get the owners to begin composting and educating the customers, as well. She felt frustrated, she said, because so many people that she talked to − including her boss − about taking better care of the earth are just not interested. She said that more often than not, they will shrug their shoulders and casually say, "Don't worry about it." So many people assume that the earth can handle anything we throw at it, on it or in it. Just like we take for granted that our body house can handle any kind of junk food that we thoughtlessly consume. We are caught up in a whirlwind of glitzy commercialism and all kinds of advanced technologies. It is time to do an about face and step out into nature's classroom and listen. You will discover that you can find a way to take care of this earth home and also enjoy those advanced tools of technology.

10

To Judge or Not to Judge, That is the Question?

Matthew 7:1-2 "Do not judge, so that you may not be judged. For with the judgment you make you will be judged, and the measure you give will be the measure you get."

This is only one of the many verses in the New Testament that deals with judgment. Of course, telling we humans not to judge is like telling a bird not to fly. We have a Radar Tower Head and judging and assessing situations is what it does. However, there are ways to let a little light shine into our Radar Tower Head windows.

Included in my own prayers is always a section on judgment. "Please, dear God, help me be less judgmental." I have to laugh, because the next thought I have will be a judgment thought. However, I now choose to listen to those thoughts and decide which are appropriate and which I want to toss onto my energetic compost pile.

Of course, we need that judgment ability to make wise choices and to keep us safe. What we don't need is the hate/ destroy/ it's got to be my way tornado judgments.

I want to share one of the most powerful and enlightening experiences that I have ever had. In January of 2009, I was traveling to the Akron area for a seminar. I left home feeling wonderful. I'd had a beautiful early morning meditation time and was looking forward to this seminar. It was snowing a little, but not bad as winter days go. I got off the Ohio Turnpike at exit 77, paid my toll and started forward, not fast because I was pulling out of a toll booth. Then the red pickup truck in front of me stopped suddenly. I slammed my brakes, but oh, no, I hit him! I jumped out of my car to have a look. The truck had a trailer hitch on the bumper so there was no damage. I had a little mark on my car but it was nothing much as I was not moving very fast. As I was pondering the situation, the man jumped out of his truck and came charging at me waving his arms and shouting. In that moment I decided to totally withdraw my feelings. I dropped right out of my Radar Tower Head, so to speak. He got right up in my face, his face red with anger. I couldn't understand all that he was saying because he was shouting in such a violent way. Finally he said, "I want your name…I want your telephone number." He then turned and stomped back to his truck. I just stood there feeling peace and quiet all around myself. He returned with paper and pencil. Still shouting he said, "What's your name?" I quietly told him. "What's your phone number?" I quietly told him. Then he said, "Do you want mine?" I said no very quietly. He stammered a bit then grabbed my right hand and shook it, still in the anger mode. He then turned and stomped off toward his truck. I could not let him go like that. I stretched out my hand to his retreating figure and softly said, "Please, would you take my hand again?" He stopped, slowly turned around, and looked at me. Then he walked back to me and took hold of my out stretched hand. When he let go of my hand, he put his arms around me and hugged me. He then turned and walked slowly back to his truck and drove off. I can't even begin to describe the feeling I was left with. All I could say was, "Thank you, dear God." I knew that I had just had an incredible lesson on judgment.

I have thought a lot about that experience. I know that if I had said to that man, even in a quiet tone of voice, "There is no damage why are you so upset?" that would have been a judgment and he would have become angrier than he was already. As I thought about him, I said to myself, "Maybe he just found out that something has happened to his son?" One of the words on his license plate was SON. "Maybe he just lost his job?" It could have been so many things. I'll never know why. The only thing I know for sure is that I chose to meet him in my Heart Territory, the place of nonjudgment and peace. I want always to remember that the extended hand of peace is more powerful than the clenched fist of force.

Before we leave this judgment section, I have another story to share with you that happened in the summer of 2005.

One of our favorite vacation places is Stratford, Canada. We love attending the Stratford Festival Theatre. Our first trip there was back in 1965. We always stay at the Forest Motel, just outside of town. Indeed, it's in a forest and is beside a wonderful lake that is the summer home to a pair of magnificent swans. The motel owners have provided tables along the lake and we love to have our breakfast there. It is a wonderful way to begin any day.

We arrived on a Friday evening in August of 2005. Early the next morning I drove over to Zehr's, one of those huge stores that has everything, to pick up food for our breakfast. Being a Saturday morning it was quite crowded. As quickly as I could, I gathered up our breakfast things and headed to the checkout area. There were long lines everywhere. I chose one of the express lanes. Right in front of me was a young couple. They had very different hard to describe hairdos, a few earrings here and there – not necessarily in their ears – and some tattoos thrown in for good measure.

My first thought was not kind. "Oh, for goodness sakes, who are they trying to impress?" I caught myself immediately and said to myself, "Laura, shame on you. They have a right to dress any way they wish and it's not your business to pass judgment on them." So, I decided to look at all of their good qualities. It was actually fun to do that. By the time we got close to the check out area, I could have invited them to breakfast. I wanted to get to know them. I noticed that he was carrying a potted plant and some potting soil and she had some odds and ends having to do with gardening. I said, "It looks like you two are going to have a busy morning in the garden." They turned around and looked down at me (they were quite tall), with a look that wasn't too kind. Sort of a "Who is this old lady interrupting us," kind of look. It was fascinating to me because the look on their faces disappeared immediately as they could feel no judgment from me. She started to laugh telling me how she was always buying new plants and he had to do all the work planting and transplanting them when they grew too big for the pots. We had a delightful conversation.

They checked out and headed for the exit as I placed my things on

the counter. I glanced toward the exit and saw her standing there looking back at me. She then ran over to me, leaned down very close and
said, "Thank you." Then she turned and ran out the door. It was totally
unexpected and very touching. In any situation we always have a choice
between the extended hand of peace or the clenched fist of force.

11
The Little Child

The New Testament has many verses about children all spoken by
the Prince of Peace, Jesus Christ. I have chosen to quote two of them.
You who have read the Bible certainly know this quote from the Be-
atitudes, *Matthew* 5:9 – "Blessed are the peacemakers, for they shall be
called the children of God." *Mark* 10:14-15 – "Let the little children
come to me; do not stop them; for it is to such as these that the kingdom
of God belongs. Truly, I tell you, whoever does not receive the kingdom
of God as a little child will never enter it."

It has been a great privilege to teach and work with children a big
part of my life. I would like to share a few observations with you having
to do with children. This goes back to the late spring of 1953. Commencement was a month away, at which time I would be receiving my
BS in Music Education from Indiana State Teachers College located in
Indiana, Pennsylvania. (The school is now called Indiana University of
Pennsylvania.)

I was chatting with some friends in a dorm room when the door
burst open and another friend entered. She was laughing and it was
obvious that she had something that she wanted to share with us. She
had just come from the lab school on campus where she had taught a first
grade class. In a month she would be receiving her degree in elementary

education. She was laughing so hard that she could hardly get the words out. Of course, we all started to laugh because she was laughing.

Finally, she was able to tell us what had happened. She was standing in front of the class sharing the lesson and everything was going well. Everyone seemed to be paying attention, but one little boy who was seated directly in front of her seemed to be especially interested. She said that he seemed totally engrossed with what she was saying. She was pleased thinking that she was doing an excellent job of teaching. Then quite unexpectedly he said to her, "You have crooked teeth." We all burst out laughing again and she as well. I'm chuckling right now recalling that experience from my college days.

Now let's think about that. If an adult would have said that to her she would have been very hurt, insulted or angry. She certainly would not have come back to the dorm laughing. It's about judgment isn't it? The child simply made an observation. This is what children do. There was no judgment with his words so of course my friend did not feel judged.

I love to watch how people respond to children. I remember a party that I attended with about 40 or so guests. As is typical with large parties, guests will get together in small groups and talk. I became aware of two men who were engaged in a very intense conversation with much hand and arm gesturing. A woman approached them carrying a little baby. Their first reaction was a look of "don't interrupt us, please, can't you see that we're talking?" Then they looked down at the baby and something magical happened. It was like watching a curtain lift from their faces revealing lovely smiles as they looked down at that small one. They were in the presence of a little child who did not know how to judge.

I love being in church when a little one is baptized. After the baptism ceremony is completed, our pastor carries the baby all around the church for everyone to see.

We who sing in the choir get to observe what happens. There is not one person who is not wearing a smile in the presence of that baby. You can feel peace, love and joy everywhere. Without realizing it, we all slide out of our Radar Tower Heads into our Heart Territories, that place of nonjudgment and peace with which we are all encoded. It is something to think about, isn't it?

12
Straitjacket or Straightjacket?

The dictionary gives us a choice of two spellings. But I say that it doesn't matter how you spell it – strait or straight – we all know what it is. A straightjacket is used when someone needs to be restrained because his or her behavior is out of control. It is used to keep that person not only from harming himself or herself, but also from harming others.

Now, I'd like you to think about an energetic straightjacket. Just where do you think you will find that kind of restriction? Certainly not in the Heart Territory, the place of peace. You guessed it, in the Radar Tower Head, of course. How does that happen? Well, for example, sometimes we become so angry or upset about a situation that has occurred we find it impossible to get a good night's sleep. We toss and turn and maybe even jump out of bed and pace the floor. Our heads are constantly chattering like the winds of a storm gathering momentum and our whole being is like a raging tornado or hurricane. It is hard to hear that gentle voice of peace in the Heart Territory when there is a straightjacket draped over our Radar Tower Head.

I'd like to call your attention to some of the ways that we humans try to put a straightjacket on this beautiful earth that we call home. I live in a rural area and drive by many farms. It makes me sad, because so many of the fields, both after harvest and before being seeded in the spring look like they have been encased in plastic. Many farmers have chosen to grow genetically modified crops (GMO). These seeds that are being used have been laced with a chemical that makes them immune to the spray the farmers use to kill the weeds in the planted fields. The corn and soy beans look tall and green but like robots, they have no "heart." I was stunned when a farmer told me that the crops harvested from the GMO plantings will not germinate. You can plant their seeds in the most fertile soil and they will not/ can not grow. I call these crops robot corn and robot soy beans.

Is this the kind of grain that I want to eat and use to feed my family and my animals? Absolutely not. I want real grain that has been grown organically. Are we throwing down the gauntlet before God, so to speak, behaving in a way that implies that we humans in our Radar Tower Heads know what is best for planet Earth?

A number of years ago I attended a natural foods convention. I will never forget a presentation that was given by a commercial farmer from Minnesota. Because of illness in his family, he had made the decision to raise his crops organically. Among other things, he told us how his crops were able to survive during a summer of draught. The soil was cared for in a way that allowed it to retain moisture until the rains came. This was not the case for the non-organic approach of farmers all around him who followed the plan of the chemical companies. This farmer that raised his crops organically, worked with the earth – no straightjackets – and the earth responded with abundance. The health of his family improved.

I know people who farm organically and have hives of honey bees.

They ask the farmers who use GMO seeds to let them know when they are going to wet spray so that they can cover their bee hives with screens until the spray dries. So many bees have died because of this spray that many orchards have to rent bee hives in the spring. Honey bees pollinate an estimated one-third of all the food crops we consume. I have seen only two honey bees on my property this summer and there was a time when they were everywhere.

I've had conversations with farmers, who have told me that they are concerned about this GMO approach, but are not sure what to do about it. They have been told that this is the only way that there will be enough to feed the hungry around the world. I know a farmer who started growing GMO crops, thinking it was the best way. He came across a bag of "real corn" that he had and, not wanting to waste it, he decided to plant it. He did not think that it would yield much of a crop, but guess what? That field yielded a bigger crop than his GMO fields. It is vital that we get out of our Radar Tower Heads and tune in to the peace frequency of the earth. This magnificent planet has the ability to feed us very well if we decide to work with it; just like our own bodies.

Yes, I am talking about that body house that I wrote about in the "Coming to Earth" chapter. We need to pay attention to what we put into our mouths if we wish to stay strong and healthy. There is certainly a wealth of information available about the importance of eating fresh fruits, vegetables and whole grains. In my opinion, it is vital to read the list of ingredients on any package of food before you put it into your grocery cart. Remember, you are buying that food for yourself and your precious family. I know that sometimes it is a challenge to find the ingredient list let alone be able to read it because the print is so small. When I have to search to find that list it arouses my curiosity. I begin to wonder if there could be something in that product that the food company doesn't want me to see. When I find something that I know is harmful it stays on the shelf. I also make a note of the 1-800 phone number on the package and I call the company when I arrive home. I encourage people to do this. Many people think that one phone call will not make a difference. I say it will if enough of us "one person at a time" people do just that. Let the customer service person know that you are concerned and that you will never buy the product that contains harmful ingredients. Not only that, let it be known that you are going to pass the word on to everyone you know. If enough of us did that and stopped buying the product that company would make a change.

We have the power within the passion of our Heart Territory to make a difference. Find out what is going on in the oil and gas industries. Check all the sources of information, not just what is being shown to you in the dazzling television commercials that are produced by the big industries. We should always check independent sources of any product that has to do with our food, water and health. In this day and age of larger than life advertising, we cannot allow ourselves to be so gullible that we go along with everything that we see in commercials. If something sounds too good to be true, it is worth checking the source. We must work with this magnificent earth if we wish to have pure water, clean air and wholesome food. We cannot continue to allow our beautiful home to be battered, fractured, bound and gagged, so that it is unable to provide the food and water that we need to survive.

Something to think about: what if in the far distant future on a faraway planet in another galaxy, the inhabitants who live there become aware of our earth? They wonder, as they study it, if it had ever been inhabited? If so, what happened? It's a sobering thought, isn't it?

Albert Einstein said: "A human being is part of the whole called by us universe, a part limited in time and space. We experience ourselves, our thoughts and feelings as something separate from the rest. A kind of optical delusion of consciousness. This delusion is a kind of prison for us, restricting us to our personal desires and to affection for a few persons nearest to us. Our task must be to free ourselves from the prison by widening our circle of compassion to embrace all living creatures and the whole of nature in its beauty. We shall require a substantially new manner of thinking if mankind is to survive."

My farmer friend recently told me that the industry has been doing research on GMO seeds, trying to get them to grow. The word is that they are having success with that. However, my friend said, "What good is it getting the seeds to grow if they are still full of harmful chemicals?" I say once a robot always a robot. Technology – no matter how clever or advanced – cannot match, duplicate or outsmart the power of the natural world.

13
Sailing Lessons

This is northern Ohio. Perhaps on lovely summer days you have enjoyed sitting on the beach watching the sailboats on Lake Erie? Then one day the idea comes to you, "I want to learn how to sail." Now you know next to nothing about sailboats and sailing so you buy a book on how to sail. In addition, you gather every bit of information that is available on the subject of sailboats and how to use them. All winter long you study everything in those books, feeling very excited about the knowledge that you are acquiring. As a matter of fact, you could get an A on an exam about sailing.

Finally the long awaited day arrives. You are filled with excitement as you travel to the dock where you will step into a sailboat for your first lesson. It is a beautiful summer day but there is hardly any breeze so the boat cannot travel very far from the dock. "Well, maybe tomorrow there will be more of a breeze," you say to yourself. Now just suppose that every day you sit in the boat the same thing happens. Think about it, could you learn to be an expert sailor? Of course not, because it is only when we are confronted by winds, waves and storms that we can really learn how to sail. The bigger the storm the more skilled we can become. Think about the storms of life. The only way we can become expert sailors on this journey of life is to embrace those storms that come up. Everyone experiences storms in this life, no one gets a free ride. You cannot hide from them no matter how hard you try.

Now back to the sailboat. If a storm comes up, we cannot let go of the sails and hide in a corner of the boat. We must become one with the storm and use all of those skills that we have learned in order to navigate through that storm. We must do the same thing when storms in our lives occur, and, in a sense become one with the storm just as you did on the sailboat. We always have a choice about how we deal with storms of life. Do we run up into our Radar Tower Head of force and huddle in a corner or do we choose to embrace that storm in our Heart Territory of power and peace? When we can throw open the shutters of our Radar Tower Head and allow the warmth of the sun to shine in on all of those fears, we will experience a profound depth of love and understanding.

I have decided to share one of my own life storm experiences with you. In February of 2010, I took my dear husband, Ron, to the emergency room where he was admitted to the hospital with pneumonia. It never entered my mind that he would not be coming back home after he recovered. He was put on oxygen in the hospital and, of course, medication to deal with the pneumonia. He had had breathing issues for quite some time having been diagnosed with pulmonary fibrosis. No one knew the degree of his difficulty in breathing because he never complained. As a matter of fact, he was a member of the church choir and no one knew how hard it was for him to breathe. However, he would often say to me after practice, "I don't know how much longer I'm going to be able to do this, Laura." He sang bass and was 6'6" tall. That's a lot to hold up when you are oxygen deprived, holding your music, and singing a powerful hymn.

After being in the hospital for just short of two weeks, the doctor came in and talked to us about interim nursing home care for Ron. He also said that Ron would need to carry oxygen with him. When the doctor left the room, I will never forget the look on Ron's face as we made eye contact. He did not say a word but his eyes told me everything. When you share lives for 50 years you do not need words to communicate. "I can't do this, Laura," his eyes told me. There was nothing that either of us could say, we were suspended in that moment by love. I knew that he had made the decision to leave. I will always be grateful that I could be with Ron and hold him in my arms as his spirit slipped quietly from his body house into that peaceful Kingdom of God. My best friend, my dear husband left this earth. I felt empty. I had no tears. There were tears and pain somewhere but I could not feel them, they were too deep.

A couple of months after Ron died, some friends invited me to go to an orchestra concert. I accepted the invitation. This was at a theatre that Ron and I had attended often. Both Ron and I loved music and theatre. I knew that I would see many friends at the concert. The performance was on a Saturday night. That morning I began to feel very anxious about the thought of walking into that theatre without Ron. How could I deal with all of those people coming up to me and asking me how I was doing? Saturday afternoon came and I began to experience severe pains deep in my lower abdominal area. I could not sit or stand still because the pains became more intense. I paced the floor. I didn't think that I could attend that concert. I knew that this pain was grief and that I was hiding in my Radar Tower Head of fear. In that moment I made the decision to face that storm of fear. I walked slowly into my favorite room and stood quietly with my arms at my sides. I took a deep breath, bent over, wrapped my arms around my belly and said with every bit of passion that I possess, "Thank you for this pain! Thank you for showing me that this is grief! Thank you! I know that out of this pain a deeper level of compassion and understanding will grow within me! Thank you!" Then I stood up very slowly and allowed my arms to drop to my sides. As I did this I could feel the pain literally drain from my body. This was one of the most profound experiences of my life. I had made the decision to stand at the helm and face that storm of life, not with fear, but with the power of my heart. I was able to attend the concert and talk with many friends that evening.

Of course, I will always miss Ron, but my grief has been composted now and has become part of the rich soil of compassion and understanding in my Heart Territory. I had always felt sympathy and compassion for women who had lost their husbands, but I didn't have a clue about how it felt until I experienced it myself.

Pain is an extraordinary teacher that has the ability to crack us open to the world of nonjudgment where we cannot even think, let alone judge. This is one of the gifts of pain. I have had the privilege of being with people who have shared with me how much the cancer in their bodies awoke them to a new understanding of the depth of life and love.

I recall a woman that I had the privilege of working with many years ago. She said, "You know, Laura, I had no idea that this cancer would be such a gift, I have learned so much." Whether pain is physical or emotional, it packs a power punch that gives us the opportunity to view life on this earth with new eyes. Like a volcano erupting, we cannot ignore it. We react and respond with no time to think. Do we hide in a corner of that life journey sailboat or do we stand at the helm and embrace that storm of life?

I have one more story to share with you, a different look at the pain process. As I have mentioned before, we lived in a rural area when I was a child. On Sunday mornings we attended a one room church that sat on top of a hill. I loved the church and have fond memories of the times we spent there. After December 7, 1941, all of the young men were being drafted and sent off to war, including pastors. Consequently, the pastor that came to serve our congregation had been retired for quite some time. His name was Pastor Woods and I will never forget him. He showed up at our home quite often, usually at supper time, and, weather permitting, he walked rather than using his car. He loved to laugh and tell stories that we loved hearing. He was our pastor for many years.

Pastor Woods was born in the 1870s, and had been raised on a farm in the plains of Nebraska. He said that he had always been very strong and healthy, never got sick and, not only that, he had never had a headache or a toothache in his life. He had no idea what pain was, never having experienced it. His conversations and stories were generally very upbeat. However, once he spoke with a very serious tone of voice. There was a veil of sadness that seemed to engulf him when he said, "It makes me sad when I visit the sick and sit at their bedsides. When they or their families tell me of the pain they are going through, I don't know what they are talking about because I have never really experienced that kind of pain." I will never forget the look on his face when he shared that.

If we sit in our life journey sailboats waiting for lessons and experience only a gentle breeze rocking the boat, how can we ever become expert sailors?

14

A Little Girl, a Grumpy Old Man and his Dog

A number of years ago a friend shared this childhood experience with me. She lived on the edge of a small town and had to walk to school. There was a section that had only one house where she said that a grumpy old man lived with his dog. He never spoke to her but would sic his dog on her if he happened to be on the porch when she was walking either to or from school. Because of this she always walked on the opposite side of the road.

She was terrified when she saw them on the porch and would run as fast as she could to reach the safe area. A number of times, she said, the dog actually got close enough to nip at her but was never quite able to bite her. One day her timing was not very good and she knew that the dog was going to get her. He had caught up with her. She felt trapped.

Suddenly, she stopped. She said that she did not know what made her do that. All fear left her as she turned and looked straight down into the dog's eyes. The dog stopped barking as he looked up at her. After a moment or two, the dog turned and trotted peacefully back to his owner. She stood there for a moment watching the dog, then she turned and walked to school. After that she said that the old man was never again able to get his dog to go after her, though he tried.

Remember the old saying that the dog bites the person who is afraid? Without realizing it, that little girl was facing her fear and learning a life lesson. She is now a grandma and told me that she will never forget that valuable experience from her grade school days.

15
Prayer Seed

We all have special memories that we carry as we travel through this life. One of my very special ones is my first piano lesson. My third grade year was special because electricity had come to the area and we now had consolidated schools in the township. This was totally different than my one room schoolhouse experience. There were two grades in each classroom. We did not have poetry read to us in this class, however. We had a traveling music teacher that came to us once a week. Mrs. Ference is another teacher that I will remember forever. It probably won't surprise you when I tell you that music became my favorite subject. It certainly wasn't math, my father could attest to that.

Oh, how I wanted to take piano lessons. However, we were still recovering from the great depression and, as much as he wanted to, my father did not have the money to buy a piano, let alone the money to pay for lessons. I have discovered that, when I hold something deep within the peace of my Heart Territory, it is like planting a prayer seed that is tucked deep within me. Like all seeds, this prayer seed quietly begins to grow and, when least expected, it blooms.

I'd like to compare this to nature's garden. We choose special seeds and we plant them in soil that we have prepared. We certainly don't hover

over the garden pacing up and down wondering if those seeds are going to grow. There is a knowing deep within us that, even as we are putting our garden tools away, those seeds are already beginning to grow. There is no force, only the power of nature and the sun.

As a child I went about my life doing the things I liked to do. I certainly did not constantly complain to my parents, "When am I going to get a piano?" That piano prayer seed had been planted and was growing, because that is what seeds do. Well guess what? A man that my father worked with said to him one day, "Do you know anyone who would like to have a piano? We have one that we want to get rid of." I am sure that you can guess what my father said. I will never forget that big old piano being carried into our house. I was in fourth grade and I thought it was beautiful. There was no money for lessons, so I taught myself how to play.

Please take a giant leap with me from fourth grade to high school. On Saturday, May 10, 1947, near the end of my sophomore year, my parents took me to Cooper Brothers Music Store in New Kensington, Pennsylvania, where I met Joy Yinger. She ushered me into her studio and invited me to have a seat at the piano. Another prayer seed was blooming deep within my heart, the seed that had been growing since I was in third grade. I couldn't hold back my tears. She was a wonderful teacher. In May of 1949, I played a Chopin polonaise at my senior commencement ceremony. In September of that year I entered music school. Before we leave this chapter, I want to share another special piano memory with you. In the late spring of 1948, I had been taking lessons for a year, and my father saw an ad in the Sunday newspaper advertising a Steinway Baby Grand for sale. Both of my parents thought it was about time that I had something better to play on than the old upright piano that had been given to us when I was in fourth grade. So that afternoon, my father, mother, my two younger sisters and I set off in the family car.

The home was in a suburb of Pittsburgh, and it took us about an hour to get there. That piano had been made in 1892, by master craftsmen. They had inlaid beautiful designs into its satin wood. I felt a deep connection to that piano, almost as if it had been waiting for me to arrive. My father said, "Yes, we'll buy it." As the woman accepted the money, she apologized because one side had been exposed to the sun coming in through the window. As a result, the finish of the piano was faded on that side. I didn't care, I thought it was the most beautiful piano that I had ever seen. I knew that this was a sacrifice for my father, however. I also knew that he and my mother were very happy to be doing this. I can't begin to tell you the joy I felt each time I played that piano. It spoke to me. Those of you who play a special instrument know what I mean, I'm sure.

We jump ahead many years to the late 1990s. My father and mother had passed away and it was time to make a decision about my piano. We had no room for it in our home, so I had to think about selling it. I did not talk about it because it was too painful. I just planted that little prayer seed deep into my Heart Territory, not knowing when or how it would bloom.

I heard about a man in Cleveland who loved to restore old pianos. I called him and told him about my piano. He was very interested and said that he would meet me at my parents home in Pennsylvania. It didn't take long for him to make me an offer. My piano was loaded onto a truck and off it went on another of its life adventures. The man said that he would contact me when the refurbishing was completed.

Two years later the long awaited day arrived. My husband and I got there at the appointed time. There it was, my piano, sitting in the showroom in all of its glory. As it turned out, the man and his craftsmen were so impressed with the piano that they decided to completely restore it. It was like it had been in 1892. The man was delighted with the piano and had no desire to sell it. This pleased me because it meant that I could visit it from time to time and feel the thrill of sitting down and placing my fingers on those beautiful keys.

Then came the day that I had hoped would never come. I walked into the showroom in early May of 2004. Everything was changed. My piano was nowhere to be seen. I felt as if I had been run over. The manager in charge told me that the owner had become very ill and had decided to sell all of his pianos. They were to be auctioned off that summer. He then led me to my piano, which was now against the wall lined up with all of the other pianos.

This life journey is amazing. As it turned out, our son and his wife-to-be arrived from California at the end of May to attend a wedding shower that was being given for them by our family friends. I asked them if they would like to go and see the piano. Our son loved the piano and had played it often in his growing up years when he visited his grandparents in Pennsylvania.

On the way, we saw a bald eagle perched high on the limb of a tree that was very close to the highway. For those of you who believe in signs from nature, this was very powerful. That eagle was a messenger of hope. When we reached the showroom, our son sat down at the piano and played. I couldn't hold back my tears. We then bid our goodbyes to the piano and returned home.

In August, my husband and I travelled to California for the wedding. There in the living room of their new home sat the piano. Our son and his wife-to-be had purchased the piano and sent it on its next adventure. It had travelled from Ohio across the country to it's new home in California. It arrived just a week before the wedding was to take place. The little prayer seed that had been quietly growing all of those years had burst into bloom in the sun of California.

There are no words that can describe the feeling that I have about that piano that I first played in the spring of 1948. It is now 2015. I know that a prayer seed never stops growing when planted deep in the soil of the Heart Territory. Who knows when this one will bloom again? Perhaps one day when one of my grandsons sits down at the piano and feels the wonder of its voice, the prayer seed will bloom.

Prayer seeds come in all varieties ready to grow and bloom when planted deep within the fertile soil of the Heart Territory.

16
The Dandelion

I told my daughter, Kim, that I was working on a chapter called "The Dandelion." She said, "The Dandelion? Why on earth would you be writing about a dandelion, Mother?" Now I realize that there are many of you who would ask the same question. Many people hate even the mention of a dandelion, let alone the sight of one growing, especially in their lawns.

A number of years ago, I asked a teenager what he thought of dandelions. He made a terrible face and said, "They're ugly!" I invited him to walk outside with me. It was spring and I had dandelions growing everywhere, so it was easy to find a large beautiful flower. I picked it and handed it to him, "Please, look closely at this flower and forget it's name for a moment. Notice all of the tiny golden petals growing out from the center. It reminds me of the sun," I said to him.

Of course, we all know that we cannot live without the sun. Nothing can live without the life-giving rays of the sun. To me the dandelion is a reminder of the sun's healing power.

I was fortunate as a child because I was never told that dandelions were something to be loathed. Quite the contrary, we ate the greens, especially in the spring. Our yards and fields were full of them. My sisters and I picked bouquets and made garlands of them. We loved blowing on the seed puffs and had contests to see who could blow them the farthest.

The dandelion blossom is one of my favorite flowers. I jump for joy when I see my first spring dandelions. I eat them almost every day during their growing season. In winter I often buy dandelion capsules from the health food store. Dandelions contain protein, calcium, magnesium, iron, potassium, choline, vitamin K and vitamin A, just to name a few of the nutrients. A friend of my dad's made wine from the flowers. You can buy dandelion tea that is made from the roots and it is delicious. If you were stranded out in the wilderness, the dandelion is so nutritious that it could save your life. It is amazing to me that this noble plant that has been used for centuries by herb doctors to help save peoples lives has become so hated.

The common name dandelion comes from the French *dent de lion*, meaning lion's tooth, because of the shape of its leaves. The English word dandelion comes from a corruption of the French word. If you look up the meaning of dandy in the dictionary it says "good, just fine." That makes me chuckle. The lion is called the king of the beasts. There is a wonderful musical called *The Lion King*, and don't forget, there was an English king called Richard, the Lionhearted. This little lionhearted dandelion gives us an incredible example of how to keep going, no matter what. I choose to call the dandelion the king of the wild plants, even though many people call it an ugly weed.

Let's go back to the young teenager that I spoke of earlier. He lived in town where every lawn looked like a green grass carpet. Weeds were a no-no, and consequently, my young friend had never heard a kind word spoken about a dandelion. He only saw them from a distance and when one was spotted, out would come the spray. How did this idea that lawns must be perfectly manicured come about? Certainly the lawn care chemical companies have contributed to this with their persuasive, larger than life advertising campaigns. These colorful commercials are very appealing to our Radar Tower Head mentalities. It becomes harder and harder to hear the voice of nature when we are surrounded by the clamor of commercialism.

However, nature is very well represented by the tiny but powerful lionhearted dandelion that does not know how to give up. The next time you see the sunny face of a little dandelion, pick the flower. Forget its name for a bit and notice all of those tiny golden petals growing out from the center. You are looking at a reminder of nature's ability to heal and give us food, Mother Earth's little sun.

17

The Lone Flower
Miracle in a Parking Lot

In August of 2011, I pulled into the parking lot of a local post office. As I got out of my car I spied a tiny red flower growing where the sidewalk joins the parking area. I ran over to it and dropped to my hands and knees to have a closer look. I was amazed with what I saw. There was no crack between the cement walk and the asphalt parking surface, nor was there any soil. How could that little flower grow and survive? The only thing that I could see was a tiny bit of dried grass. Somehow that little seed had been blown from the flower garden beside the post office and found enough nourishment in that a bit of dried grass that nature had composted. It was bright, beautiful and healthy, oblivious of that cement/ asphalt barrier. I didn't bother going into the post office, but ran back to my car and drove home to get my camera. How can we ever feel that there is no hope when we observe the miracle of nature all around us?

18
The Dance of Life Goes On

In 1989, I received my Ohio State Medical Board License to begin a new profession as a massage therapist. When I entered massage therapy school many of my friends thought that I had gone off the deep end, so to speak. My husband told me later that he thought it was just a whim that would pass. However, he changed his mind when he realized what this work was all about and how much it meant to me.

After successfully completing the required classes at the school, I was eligible to take the State Board exam to obtain a license to practice massage therapy in Ohio. With my license framed and hanging on the wall of my office, I began my new profession. I was totally engaged from day one.

The basic study at the school was very good, but I knew that I would never be content with just that. I wanted to learn everything I could about body work. I have studied CranioSacral Therapy, Lymph Drainage Techniques, SomatoEmotional Release, Myofacial Release, Neuromuscular Therapy, Reike, and Foot Reflexology to name a few. I feel extremely blessed to have had phenomenal teachers.

This profession requires "listening" with your hands, for lack of a better way to explain it. When you first begin the work, the tendency is to think that you can fix the client that comes in complaining about a sore back or aching muscles. Certainly we have learned techniques to do that. However, with experience and advanced study I realized that there is much more to it than that. I compare this to becoming a teacher.

I certainly discovered when I began to teach that you cannot make a child learn. The really fine teachers, in my opinion, are passionate about the subjects that they teach and, as a result, the children cannot help but respond and learn. These teachers work from the power of the Heart Territory rather than the force of the Radar Tower Head.

I'd like to give you an example that goes back to my freshman year in college. Though I was a music student, I was required to take some classes that had nothing to do with music. One of them was called physical science. I earned a D in that class, which was not really a surprise since I don't remember ever opening the book. I had to go to summer school and take the class again. The teacher's name was Dr. Reiber. With a big smile and great energy, he walked to the front of the classroom and began speaking as if he had something wonderful to share. He got my attention immediately. Even though this was not a subject that interested me, I grew to love it because of the joy and passion of Dr. Reiber. He made all of the information interesting and easy to understand. On the last day of class Dr. Reiber began telling us about the next level of physical science and his description sounded so exciting I almost signed up for it. Thank goodness, I caught myself in the nick of time. I was a music student, this was not for me. For Dr. Reiber, teaching was not a job, it was his passion. He was teaching from the same place that the great musician, artist or writer creates masterpieces. Whatever class you take, you must learn all of the techniques and principles that the instructor presents. I am not going to talk to you about the specifics of each therapy that I have studied, that is not my purpose here. I certainly have a completely different perception of massage therapy now than I did in 1989. We all learn and grow with experience, especially with something that we are passionate about. I approach this with the same joy and commitment that I have when I am working in the drama and music fields. Massage therapy is a healing art.

After receiving my license, I enrolled in Neuromuscular Therapy classes. The teacher was excellent and I am grateful to have had the opportunity to attend a seminar at each level of his work, which included amazing demonstrations. The next therapies that I studied required very light touch. I began with CranioSacral Therapy, which has been described as a semi-closed hydraulic system having to do with the production, circulation and reabsorption of the cerebrospinal fluid. We learned to feel that movement all over the body. It is truly amazing. Each system of the body has its own rhythm and function.

These gentle touch therapies have reminded me of the connection that I have always felt within nature. As far back as I can remember, I was aware of nature's voice. I felt it in everything. I spent much of my young life in trees and have always talked and listened to them with my hands. As a matter of fact I still do. On a Sunday morning in the late 80s, shortly after we moved into this house, we had gone to the early church service. My husband had to stay for both services to attend a special meeting, so I came home after the first service. It was in the late fall and the leaves had fallen from the trees. It was raining hard and a strong wind was blowing. I went into the house and hurried back to the room that was closest to the woods. I stood by the window watching the trees that were being tossed about by the strong wind. My eyes connected with one of the trees. I had the feeling that it was going to fall. From deep within my heart I said to the tree, reaching my hands toward it, "I know that you may have to fall, please protect my space." I had hardly gotten the words out of my mouth when the tree broke off about five feet up from its base and fell toward me. It fell just short of the house. Had it not broken off where it did, it would have hit the house and done considerable damage. Needless to say, I thanked the tree and, when the rain stopped, I went outside and wrapped my arms around its trunk with much gratitude.

Following the CranioSacral study, I attended SomatoEmotional Release seminars. This is a therapeutic process that helps rid the mind and body of the residual effects of past trauma associated with negative experiences. In all of these classes the instructor needs a class member to come forward so that he or she can demonstrate the techniques involved in the therapy. I had no idea what to expect when I got on the therapy table. As the instructor began, much to my surprise, I could not hold back my tears as a memory came to me of a traumatic event that had occurred when I was in eight grade. When I was born I was named Laura Elizabeth after both of my grandmothers. I never knew that because everyone called me Betty. It was not until the end of my seventh grade year that my mother told me that Betty was a nickname for Elizabeth.

She said that she had always loved the name Betty so that was what I was called. I was pleased to know that I was Elizabeth, however I still did not know about the Laura part. At the end of my eighth grade year my parents told me that my name was Laura Elizabeth because it would be printed on my diploma.

I could hardly wait until we got home after the graduation ceremony so that I could open my diploma. We stopped first at my Grandmother Laura's house to show her. I was excited as I untied the ribbon expecting to see written for the first time in my life, Laura Elizabeth Miller. Much to my surprise I saw Rachel Elizabeth Miller. My parents were speechless and so was I. Grandmother Laura looked at it and burst into tears saying, "You hate my name…You have always hated my name." She continued to cry. I couldn't speak……..I wasn't capable of saying a word at that moment.

My dad called the school office the next day and told them about the error. Life went on as usual, however the emotional pain of that experience was buried deep within me. In a few days I received a new diploma with my name on it. I would have loved having everyone call me Laura when I entered high school but Betty had been "energetically tattooed" on me. As a matter of fact, if you look through any of my high school yearbooks you will see Betty Miller printed under all of my pictures. It is as if I never existed. When I went off to college however, it was as Laura Elizabeth Miller. My parents and sisters broke the Betty habit and started calling me Laura. They were the only ones who did, with the exception of my best friend, Marion. To everyone else who knew me in my youth I was and still am Betty. In that SomatoEmotional Release class the trauma of that diploma incident at my Grandmother Laura's house was lifted from me.

The more experienced I become with using these light touch therapies the more I realize that it is not my business to fix anyone but to lend a hand, so to speak. It is about listening with your hands and feeling the gentle movements throughout the body. I recall a preconcert talk given by the concertmaster of the Cleveland Orchestra quite a few years ago. Among other things, he talked about testing acoustics. He said that the soft tones have the most color and resonance.

Thinking about the concertmaster's observations triggers the memory of an especially powerful Cleveland Orchestra Concert that my husband and I attended quite a few years ago. The house lights dimmed and the conductor entered. After acknowledging the applause, he turned slowly and stepped onto the podium. As he gently lifted the baton, the entire orchestra positioned their instruments, becoming one with the conductor's movement. Soft tones of music like an unseen gossamer web of sound floated out over the entire concert hall and musicians, conductor and audience became one. The music ended as gently as it had begun and for a few moments everyone remained suspended in the stillness and healing peace of the Heart Territory. On cue from the conductor laying down the baton, the audience burst into applause.

The following experience quite a few years ago absolutely confirmed for me, beyond any shadow of a doubt, that our bodies respond to everything we think and say. It happened with one of my clients of many years. Among other things, she'd had breast cancer and had to have her left breast removed. She'd had an implant that was not satisfactory so that also was removed, and she had quite a bit of scar tissue in that area. Consequently, she had lymph problems in her left arm, shoulder and chest. She was a very positive woman, with a smile always on her face.

This particular day, as usual, she went into my office, disrobed and got under a large towel that covered her. I came in and placed a pillow under her knees for more comfort. Before I begin a treatment I like to hear about any special concerns. I was standing on her left side with one hand resting gently on her knee, which was covered with the towel, and my other hand on her arm. She had an unusually serious expression on her face as she moved her right arm across her body and placed her hand on the breast area that was so scarred. With anger, she said, "Laura, this is nasty!" I was not prepared for what I felt. Her body recoiled as if it had been lashed with a whip. It wasn't anything that could be seen; it was a response from deep within her body, her body responding to her anger.

I could not hold back my tears as I blurted out, "Don't say that!" It was like the response that you would have if you witnessed someone suddenly beating a child or an animal. She looked at me in surprise. Needless to say, I had never raised my voice when I was with her let alone shed tears. I then told her what I had felt in her body and suggested that during the session she apologize and send love and gratitude to every part of her body. It was a profound session, unlike any other that we had had. Since that experience, I suggest to my clients when they get on the massage table that they send love and gratitude to every part of the body. This has produced amazing results.

There are many books that have been written about the power of positive thinking and spontaneous healing.

Two years ago I found this book that had been published in1989, called *The Secret Life of Your Cells* by Robert B. Stone, Ph.D., which features, among other things, the research and experiments of Cleve Backster with both plant and human cells. I had been aware of his experiments with plants, but I didn't realize that he was working with human cells as well. He discovered in attaching a lie-detector to the leaf of a plant that it had feelings and the ability to respond to our thoughts. There are many experiments that show that our cells do react to our feelings and emotions.

One of the reasons that I love Stone's book is because it mentions the work and research of many scientists and doctors, as well as a patient's ability to heal from a serious disease. Norman Cousins, editor of the *Saturday Review of Literature*, when diagnosed as having a terminal disease, holed up with laugh tapes, comic books, and other sources of humor, and laughed himself well.

Plant geneticist, Dr. Derald Langham, in 1939 accepted a position in Venezuela to develop strains of sesame that would help make that country become more self-sufficient. For his efforts, he received the highest decoration ever given to a foreigner – and sesame remains the leading cash crop in Venezuela today. Langham said that he owed his success to the fact that, as a boy, he could stand silently by a tree, close his eyes, and sense everything around him, even birds flying above. He used this same skill with the sesame.

I was delighted to see that Bernie S. Siegel, MD was included in this book. He was a member of the Yale University faculty in New Haven, Connecticut, and became president of the American Holistic Medical Association in 1988. In 1986, his first book, *Love, Medicine & Miracles*, was published. In it he relates case after case where patients who change from an attitude of hopelessness to one of hopefulness reversed the course of their disease, even cancer. I found out about him in the late 80s when my friend, who lived in Connecticut, made an appointment with him. I have some of his lectures that were recorded on audio cassettes, and some of his books – all of which are very uplifting.

I end this chapter with my favorite Emily Dickinson poem.

"Hope" is the thing with feathers –
That perches in the soul –
And sings the tune without the words –
And never stops – at all –
And sweetest – in the Gale – is heard –
And sore must be the storm –
That could abash the little Bird
That kept so many warm –
I've heard it in the chillest land –
And on the strangest Sea –
Yet, never, in Extremity,
It asked a crumb – of Me.

19
The Voice of Trees - The Circle of Life

I stand in a large wooden pavilion in a clearing in a forest in the Berkshire Mountains of New York. I am the first person to arrive for study this morning and am not prepared for the wave of sadness that engulfs me as I place my feet on this strong wooden floor. I am reminded of how we depend on nature for everything, of how much we take for granted that trees are cut down so that we can live a comfortable life. The ache in my heart persists as I ponder the disregard for the life of nature so prevalent today. I cannot help but wonder how many people who come to this place this morning will honor the trees sacrificed so that we can be sheltered. There are those who say, "Nature is here to serve us, we two-leggeds who inhabit this earth." There are those who say, "All forms of life are sacred and we must be the voice for that which cannot speak." I feel these wooden planks beneath my feet and choose, in this moment, to be the voice of trees.

> These trees,
> nailed in place beneath my feet,
> once stood tall,
> a part of forests green,
> anchored firmly in the Mother,
> stretching upward to the sky.

Free to dance with changing seasons,
raging storms and winds of winter
subdued by April's waltz
donned in shades of palest green.

Changing partners once again
in June's seductive dance
with warmest rain, insistent sun
the full-leafed summer begun.

Perhaps this dance will never end –
but tints of gold and orange remind us
nothing ever stays the same.
And so the trees with wild abandon
surround us all and autumn reigns
with colors bright like Gypsy dancers,
the trees are poised for one last dance
before winter blankets all.

These wooden planks beneath my feet
draw in sadness to think
of those who walk the earth,
heeding not the dance of life.

How many like these pinioned trees,
are nailed in boxes marked with fear,
afraid to dance the dance of life
from birth to death, and even after?

The circle of life, – the dance of seasons, –
connects us all to the love of God,
that judges not
but gives us wonder to observe.
If we can step with quiet
out of our boxes marked with fear.

Stand beside a stately tree,
feel its pulse of life.
Feel the life that holds no judgement.
Such a quiet lesson that all of nature teaches,
dancing through the changing seasons.

What could happen if, together
with one pulse, we all united,
honoring the love we share
instead of hate and fear and doubt
that are tearing all our lives apart.

I move now from the floor to forest,
my feet connect with Mother Earth.
I feel the pulse – the dance of life –
and love that God has given.
I lift my arms without fear.
The God of love is present here
for all see and feel and know.

And so, the circle of life continues,
the dance of life that never ends.
It is our choice which dance we choose,
we cannot say, "I'll sit this out."
We must dance, we must choose
to dance with joy or hatred,
to dance with hope or fear.

And so the circle of life continues.
The choice is ours.
The dance goes on.